SCHIRMER PERFORMANCE EDITIONS

HAL LEONARD PIANO LIBRARY

THE CLASSICAL ERA
Intermediate Level

Compiled and Edited by Richard Walters

AUDIO ACCESS INCLUDED
Recorded Performances Online

Recorded by

Elena Abend
Jeffrey Biegel
Matthew Edwards
Stefanie Jacob
Jennifer Linn

To access companion recorded performances online, visit:
www.halleonard.com/mylibrary

Enter Code
7815-7882-1955-8352

On the cover:
La Camargo Dancing (c. 1730)
by Nicolas Lancret (1690–1743)

ISBN 978-1-4803-3823-4

G. SCHIRMER, Inc.

DISTRIBUTED BY
HAL•LEONARD®
CORPORATION
7777 W. BLUEMOUND RD. P.O. BOX 13819 MILWAUKEE, WI 53213

www.musicsalesclassical.com
www.halleonard.com

T0050655

CONTENTS

Though the table of contents appears in alphabetical order by composer, the music in this book is in progressive order.

The music in this collection has been edited by the compiler/editor Richard Walters, except for the pieces previously published in other volumes in the Schirmer Performance Editions series:

Beethoven: German Dance in G Major; German Dance in C Major; German Dance in B-flat Major
from *Beethoven: Selected Piano Works*
edited and recorded by Matthew Edwards

Clementi: Sonatina in F Major
from *Clementi: Sonatinas, Opus 36*
edited and recorded by Jennifer Linn

Dussek: Sonatina in G Major
from *Sonatina Album*
edited and recorded by Jeffrey Biegel

Kuhlau: Sonatina in C Major
from *Kuhlau: Selected Sonatinas*
edited and recorded by Jennifer Linn

Mozart: Piece for Clavier in F Major; Andantino in E-flat Major; Rondo in C Major; Adagio for Glass Harmonica; Funeral March for Signor Maestro Contrapunto; German Dance in C Major
from *Mozart: 15 Intermediate Piano Pieces*
edited and recorded by Elena Abend

COMPOSER BIOGRAPHIES
AND
PERFORMANCE NOTES

It is likely that the commentary below will not be read through as a whole, but only in reference to a specific composer or piece. Therefore, many ideas stated regarding Classical Era style are repeated many times.

A few general comments about Classical era style:

- Music of the Classical period will risk sounding dull if the musician does not apply insightful articulation, which alongside clarity and steadiness, is an essential component of Classical style.

- The default touch is *portato*, playing notes without indication of articulation with a slight separation.

- Legato touch generally should only be applied to notes marked with a slur.

- Articulation is part of the music and should be learned along with notes and rhythms from the beginning of practice.

- The sustaining pedal should generally not be used.

- Classical Era music is excellent for developing a refined tone and touch.

CARL PHILIPP EMANUEL BACH
German composer.
Born in Weimar, March 8, 1714;
died in Hamburg, December 14, 1788.

Carl Philipp Emanuel Bach, second son of Johann was a major composer bridging the murky distinctions between late Baroque and Early Classical periods employing a voice tied with the epithet *empfindsamer Stil* (sensitive style), meaning an emotionally turbulent or dynamically expressive compositional style as distinguished from the more restrained rococo. He was the second son of the composer Johann Sebastian Bach. As such, Carl received music lessons from his father until he began studies in law at Leipzig University and continued in Frankfurt. After graduation, Carl accepted a position in the court orchestra of Crown Prince Frederick of Prussia and moved to Berlin. In 1768 Bach became the music director of sacred music for the city of Hamburg, a position previously held by his godfather, Georg Philipp Telemann. Throughout his life, Bach was extraordinarily prolific, writing over 1,000 works for voices and keyboard instruments.

Solfeggietto in C minor, H. 220
CPE Bach generally wrote in the more "modern" *stile galante*, not the contrapuntal high Baroque of his famous father Johann Sebastian Bach. However, in this Solfeggieto from 1766, he harkens back to the earlier Baroque style. Most of the piece has a single note sounding at a time, with running sixteenth notes that outline harmonic movement. The implied harmony generally changes every two beats, on beats 1 and 3. For instance, in the first measure the implied harmony is C minor followed by G major. For dramatic effect, at the climax of the piece (measures 21–24) the composer stops changing the harmony every two beats and instead sustains the harmony through the entire measure. The technical challenge is to pass the sixteenth notes from hand to hand and maintain absolute evenness in touch and rhythm. This can only be accomplished by first practicing slowly. A listener should not be able to tell which hand is playing at any given moment. Because of the nature of this music we recommend slow practice, hands together rather than hands separately. As you master the piece begin to increase the tempo, but make sure that whatever tempo you play remains steady throughout. Do not rush this music, a tendency of student pianists in playing quick moving notes. It would be a terrible mistake to use any pedal in places where only one note at a time is played. Though a valid approach would be to use no pedal throughout the entire piece, some pianists may

wish to experiment with light pedal, with the half notes and whole notes in the bass line as a signal for pedaling.

LUDWIG VAN BEETHOVEN
German composer and pianist.
Born in Bonn, December 16, 1770;
died in Vienna, March 28, 1827.

Beethoven was the major figure of the transition from the Classical Era to the Romantic Era in music. As one of the first successful freelance composers, as opposed to a composer thriving in a royal court appointment, Beethoven wrote widely in nearly every genre of his day, with emphasis on instrumental music. He acquired wealth and fame beyond any composer before him. Beethoven's chamber music, piano sonatas, concertos and symphonies are part of the ever present international repertoire. In his youth he was regarded as one of the greatest pianists of his time, but he stopped performing after hearing loss set in. He devoted an enormous amount of his compositional efforts to the piano, which as an instrument came of age during his lifetime. He was occasionally a piano teacher, with wealthy patrons and young prodigies begging for lessons, though this task was not a match for his nature. However, teaching piano did inspire him to write many pieces for students. Because his piano music is so widely spread across the level of difficulty from easy to virtuoso, Beethoven's piano music is played by students and professional pianists.

German Dance in G Major, WoO 8, No. 6
The rustic quality to this dance gives it the feeling of a ländler. The composer has given us no tempo; this is open for interpretation. We recommend *allegro moderato*. The pianist on the companion recording takes a tempo that probably is as fast as this piece should be played. A slower tempo is certainly possible. The secret to finding the right tempo for you as you work up to a performance are the figures in measures 13–15. The tempo at which you can play these measures smoothly and without struggle is as fast as you should play the entire piece. By nature a dance is a rhythmic piece of music. Rhythm need to be steady, certainly, but there are also things about the music which emphasize rhythm, particularly articulation. Notice the variety of articulation, dynamics, and accents. We recommend no pedal to allow for clarity of execution. Note particularly the changes between the smooth phrasing of the trio and the staccato chords that come in the section before it.

German Dance in C Major, WoO 8, No. 7
Sometimes it is amazing to stop and realize that a great composer like Beethoven wrote pieces especially for piano students, such as this dance. This is music with character and high spirits. It moves from elegance, such as in the long phrases in the opening, to boisterous rambunctiousness in the section around measure 25. A pianist's ability to play a smooth scale and arpeggio will be put to the test in this music. Style comes from articulation, as is true in all Classical Era pieces. Note the sharp and sudden changes in dynamics. There are no gradual *crescendos* or *decrescendos*. Tempo is open to interpretation since Beethoven provided no tempo. An acceptable tempo might range from quarter note = 130 to 168. Whatever tempo you choose, be sure to keep it steady throughout.

German Dance in B-flat Major, WoO 13, No. 2
This dance is akin to the third movement minuet and trio, or scherzo and trio, of a Classical symphony. The music is in three large sections, the second section being the trio that begins in measure 17. The texture also reflects this ABA form, with page one being boisterous and articulated with many short notes played *f*, and page two being played *legato* and softly. The *marcato* markings in the right hand in the first few measures are a period indication of *staccato* that is pronounced and with accent. The first four measure phrase is answered in measures 5–8 with a sudden drop in dynamics and short, gentle phrases in the right hand melody. The dynamic suddenly increases to *ff* with the pickup to measure 9, but without the spiky texture of the opening phrase. Notice the detail in articulation in this section (measures 9–16). In contrast, the trio needs to be played with elegant smoothness. This piece should probably be played without pedal, allowing the fingers to accomplish all articulation clearly. Tempo must remain absolutely steady throughout. Beethoven gave no tempo indication, which leaves this open for interpretation. We have recommended *allegro moderato* because of the character of the music.

MUZIO CLEMENTI
Italian composer, pianist, teacher, publisher, and piano manufacturer.
Born in Rome, January 23, 1752;
died in Evesham, March 10, 1832.

By age 13 Clementi was organist at San Lorenzo in Rome. Peter Beckford heard the youth and brought him to study at his English estate for the next seven years. Clementi then moved to London, where performing and publishing propelled him to embark on a series of concert tours from 1780–1785. During one of these tours he entered a duel with Mozart, determining who was the better keyboard player, an evening's amusement organized by Emperor Joseph II. The contest was declared a tie. Clementi acquired many famous piano students all over Europe during his travels, including Carl Czerny, John Field, and Frédéric Chopin. Returning to London in 1785, he continued to teach some of the wealthiest and most-talented pianists of his day, and amassed enough capital to invest in music publishing and piano manufacturing. In 1802 he began another European tour, not only concertizing, but promoting his pianos and signing composers to his publishing company, including the young Beethoven. From 1810 until his death, Clementi ran his publishing company and piano manufacturing company, and made some unsuccessful attempts at symphonic writing. His piano sonatas and sonatinas (written for his piano students) were his most popular compositions during his life and remained so after his death.

Sonatina in F Major, Op. 36, No. 4

The biggest dangers of student performances of Clementi sonatinas are lack of attention to details of dynamics and articulation, an unsteady tempo, and the unwise or over use of pedal. Clementi sonatinas are perfect pieces for student pianists, but they leave a pianist's technique exposed. All details of whether you can play scales evenly, whether you have mastered tone, and whether you can maintain a tempo that neither slows down nor speeds up are all exposed. The classic approach to practice is to play hands separately at a slow tempo, observing all dynamics and articulations. Then move on to slow practice of a section at a time with hands together. This slow practice is not only about getting your fingers and muscle memory in gear. You should listen very carefully and ask yourself, "Am I playing all the articulation (phrasing, staccato and accents) as the composer has written them?" *These articulations are part of the music*, not an addition to the music. They should be learned from the earliest stages of practice, along with correct notes and rhythms. In the Classical period there is often an accompaniment figure in one hand. This is evident in the first movement in the left hand pattern of eighth note octaves. Often in quicker moving tempos, these accompaniment figures are not marked with articulation. This

leaves the pianist to apply some appropriate style. In the figure in question at the beginning of the piece, we recommend a light bounce with each note lightly articulated. In measure 13 in the left hand accompanying figure one could apply the same approach. Another choice a pianist might make is to clearly articulate two note slurs on each beat. Yet another choice for an accompaniment figure of moving eighth notes is to play smoothly. This might be the approach in measures 34–37. The implication in discussing the articulation of accompaniment figures is that you must be aware that the right hand and the left hand have individual and independent articulation. For many pianists the right hand section beginning in measures 37–41 might be the most challenging part of the piece. These sixteenth notes must be absolutely even. There is also an implied voice leading, with the lower note of the figure outlining a melody.

For the second movement Clementi states a tempo marking of *andante con espressione*. There could be a quite a range of what that tempo means. The pianist on the companion recording has interpreted it to mean quite a slow tempo, which is certainly acceptable. One could imagine this *andante* being interpreted a bit faster, with a quarter note = c. 64. In the Classical period *con espressione* does not mean the same things as it does in the Romantic period. There is a limit to how much emotion should be added to the performance. *Con espressione* does not mean rubato or deviation in tempo in the Classical Era. It usually means subtle increases and decreases in volume (known as hairpins). Some of these are marked. A student pianist must learn the discipline of playing something slower and softer with rhythmic trueness and crispness. Creating Classical style requires sculpting sharp details, even in slower music. All of the things approached in faster music, such as clarity of detail, attention to articulation, and careful attention to dynamic changes, must be applied in slower music as well. Do not allow your performance of this second movement to become mushy, with no firm definition. Force yourself to practice without pedal. Experiment in moving toward a performance using the least amount of pedal you can, with your ears as your guide. Make sure that the tone of your playing is gentle and refined, but firmly defined.

The third movement *Allegro vivace* is the most challenging of the sonatina. Many student pianists, when playing a sonata or sonatina, learn the movements in order, with the third movement coming last. This is perhaps not the best approach. It might be best, in this case, to work on this rondo first and master it before tackling the other movements. Then you will have tackled the hardest part of the sonatina first. As a result, this rondo will benefit from the longest amount of practice time, from when you begin practicing the sonatina to the time of performance. The biggest challenge in this third movement is the relentless appearance of the sixteenth note triplet figure passing from hand to hand. This must be absolutely even everywhere. A musical challenge is the witty fading off in measure 11 followed by the rests. It is as if the composer has written in for you a little acting exercise, asking you to interrupt your playing with some distraction. Use no pedal in this movement. This movement will obviously need to begin with slow practice, hands alone. This is when you should firmly decide on your fingering. As practice continues you start to build the feel of the music into your hand and into your muscle memory. This is also when you should learn the articulation that the composer has asked of you. *Articulation is part of the composition; it needs to be learned from the beginning, not added on like cake decoration after the cake is baked.* As you are learning details of articulation in this or any other piece, it does not hurt for you to exaggerate the details first. Exaggerate the details that the composer (or editor) has asked as you learn them. Then as you live with them, tastefully temper them into building the whole of your performance.

ANTON DIABELLI
Austrian publisher and composer.
Born in Mattsee, September 5, 1781;
died in Vienna, April 7, 1858.

Diabelli worked as a proofreader for S.A. Steiner & Company in Vienna while teaching piano and guitar. His interest in music publishing grew as several of his arrangements and compositions appeared in print. In 1818 he established the firm Cappi & Diabelli with a business partner. They came to publish arrangements of larger works for piano and small chamber ensembles for in home use. (In this era a piano was common in every middle and upper class home.) Later, the firm became a more serious publisher of concert music, signing composers such as Schubert and Beethoven. The name Diabelli is usually associated with Beethoven and his opus 120 variations. The publisher, as part of a marketing scheme, solicited various composers throughout Austria to write a variation on the waltz theme to be published together in one volume. Most submitted a light, short variation. However, Beethoven submitted over 30 variations. Beethoven's set was published as Volume 1, the variations by the other 50 composers as Volume II. Diabelli's music is not often performed today, with the exception of a few teaching pieces such as this sonatina from opus 168. (This opus number might be familiar to fans of the 1958 Marguerite Duras novella *Moderato Cantabile*.)

Sonatina in C Major, Op. 168, No. 3
There is a playful quality to Diabelli's sonatina that reminds one of Haydn. Wit in music is communicated through sharply sculpted details of articulation and a playful spirit. If you play this piece without attention to the articulation Diabelli has composed, you will miss the character of the music.

Practice slowly, hands separately in the first movement, learning the articulation and dynamics along with the notes and rhythms in the early stages of practice. The driving theme of the piece is the rhythmic statement at the beginning. This rhythm appears in various ways throughout. The composer marks *tenuto* over notes in measures 2, 4, 10, 12, and other places. In the eighteenth century a *tenuto* was an indication that the note should be held to its full value rather than abbreviating it by a separation before the next event. Playing slightly detached, except for notes deliberately marked in slurs, is the norm in this period. Pianists brought up to believe that *legato* playing (with every note smoothly held until the next note) is the norm have a difficult time adjusting to this and finding the style of the period. In practical terms, in this instance, indicate that you think of the notes under the *tenuto* as slurred to the next note. *In this historical period* tenuto *markings do not mean to hold the notes longer in value*, which became the meaning of *tenuto* in the nineteenth century. The accompaniment figures in the left hand must be generally smooth and quiet. This is true of eighth note patterns such as measures 9–19, and also the triplet figure in measures 47–53. Retain a steady beat throughout and use no pedal.

Most of the time, movements of a sonata or sonatina do not share thematic material. However, Diabelli begins this second movement (Andantino) with the same rhythmic theme from the first movement. This is not like most second movements in three movement works. It is not of an expressive and warm mood. The wit established in the first movement remains and is active in the second movement as well. This comes through in the crisp articulation and the sudden changes in dynamics, such as the sudden *f* in measure 8 followed by an immediate *crescendo* to a surprise *p*. This happens again in measure 16. Among the articulations Diabelli asks of the pianist are slurred staccatos, such as in the first full measure. These are short notes with a sense of phrase to them. In other words, short notes that are not single events, but shaped in the slur as marked. They are also not as short as an un-slurred staccato would be, such as the right-hand notes in measures 13 and 14. Do not use pedal and retain a steady beat, except for in the one marked *rit.* in measure 20.

The rondo theme occurs three times in this third movement Allegro: the first few measures (and its repetition), measures 41–48, and a variation in measures 69–77. This is lively music that has the spirit of a can-can dance. In faster music, student pianists often tend to speed up as the movement goes along. Guard against this! You want to create liveliness and energy, but do not want the movement sound as if it is running away from you. As with all fast music, practice first hands alone, *learning the articulation and the dynamics from the beginning, along with the correct notes and rhythms.* Then being to practice hands together slowly, small sections at a time. You should use no pedal in this movement. Do not rush through the fermata in measure 68. Part of the fun of the piece is taking this surprise break and relishing the "suspended" moment. The witty spirit that Diabelli established in the first two movements becomes most manic in this movement. This is the most challenging section of this sonatina. If you are playing the entire sonatina, we recommend learning the third movement first, so that it will benefit from the most practice time during your preparation for performance.

JAN LADISLAV DUSSEK
Bohemian pianist and composer.
Born in Čáslav, February 12, 1760; died in Saint Germain-en-Laye (or Paris), March 20, 1812.

Dussek learned music from an early age and was an impressive young musician. He dropped out of the University of Prague and began teaching and concertizing as a pianist throughout northern Europe and Russia. Dussek fled Russia upon a groundless suspicion that he was involved in a plot to assassinate Catherine II. More concertizing on the glass harmonica and piano brought him to Paris, where he remained until the French Revolution forced him on to London. He remained in London eleven years teaching and playing. He married and began a publishing business with his father-in-law. When the business failed, he left his father-in-law in debtor's prison, abandoned his wife and young daughter, and escaped to Hamburg, where he continued to play and helped to develop a six-octave piano. To show off this novelty, he performed with the piano turned sideways to the audience, a tradition that continues today. His compositions are little-remembered, with the exception of a few piano sonatinas which remain a staple of student pianists' repertoire.

Sonatina in G Major, Op. 20, No. 1
Your performance will sparkle if you pay attention to all details of articulation and dynamics. In the first movement, note the *marcato* accents, such as the first notes in the right hand in measure 2. These are different from the staccato markings in measures 17 and 19, which are played to be played with much lighter touch. Learn each hand separately, practicing slowly and *applying articulation and dynamics from the beginning as you learn the music.* The repeated notes in measures 1–3 in the left hand require steadiness and evenness. The fast sixteenth note accompaniment, such as in measures 5–7 and elsewhere, will need much practice. You must create this bed of busyness with smoothness and elegance. Do not use pedal anywhere in this movement. Practicing scales along with this sonatina will help you in playing sixteenth notes evenly, such as in measures 4, 16 and elsewhere. Though the composer does not indicate it, it would be stylistically appropriate to include a slight *diminuendo* into the final chord of the piece.

A sonatina is an abbreviated sonata. In this case, the composer has skipped the second movement, moving straight to the final movement, this Allegretto - Tempo di Minuetto. This rondo is interesting in that it is in the spirit of a minuet. Most rondos are at a faster tempo and are not minuets. We suggest that you break the piece into sections for practice, since it is a longer movement. For instance, your practice session might be broken into four sections. Section 1: measures 1–16; section 2: measures 16–38; section 3: measures 38–78; section 4: measures 79–end. Each section can be practiced hands alone, applying articulations and dynamics in the early stages of learning the music so that they become an organic part of what you have learned. Then put hands together slowly as you are practicing each section, retaining what you have absorbed about the details. The sixteenth note accompanying figure occurs a great deal in the left hand. This needs to be smooth, even and elegant. The sixteenth notes in the right and must also be very even, such as the running sixteenth note that begins measure 16. You must retain a steady tempo throughout the movement. Practice with no pedal, and probably perform this movement with no pedal as well, allowing your playing to be as clear as possible.

FRANZ JOSEPH HAYDN

Austrian composer.
Born in Rohrau, March 31, 1732;
died in Vienna, May 31, 1809.

One of the major composers of the eighteenth century, Haydn defined the sound of the Classical style. He was employed by the Esterházy court for the majority of his career, serving two Princes from the Hungarian ruling family in Vienna as well as Hungary. Later in his life, Haydn spent time in London composing for the German violinist and musical impresario Johann Peter Salomon (1745–1815). Haydn lived his last years in Vienna. He wrote in nearly every genre of his day including, most famously, operas, symphonies, and chamber music. Though his keyboard music is not as well-known as his orchestral works, he wrote over 50 piano sonatas and a large assortment of other keyboard pieces. Haydn's influence in Classical Era music is captured in the pet name by which he became known in his later life, "Papa Haydn," a term of endearment bestowed upon him by the hundreds of musicians who had learned from him. The nickname also refers to Haydn being the compositional father of the modern symphony.

Allegro from Sonata in C Major, Hob. XVI/1

This *Allegro* from Haydn makes frequent use of ornaments, such as the mordent in measure 1 and the turn in measure 22. Many students tend to learn pieces without ornamentation and add it as a final touch, or ignore it completely. Sometimes this approach makes sense, but in this little piece

you will find the style of this piece best if you learn the ornaments from the beginning. In this case, they are easy to figure out. The mordent in measure 1 (beat 1) recurs many times. It is always begun on the beat, not before the beat. It begins on the principal note and then quickly moves to the lower note and back up. Ornaments such as this at this tempo are played quickly. You can see the realization written out in small notes above the right hand for the turn in measure 22. This too is played quickly. The only other ornamentation in the piece is a trill in measure 45. This should begin on the note above. In this case, begin on E and trill the notes E and D. If you learn the ornamentation from the beginning as you slowly practice hands separately, it becomes an organic part of this *allegro*. Practice this music slowly, hands separately, with ornamentation and articulation applied. The left hand accompaniment pattern also requires attention. It should be played inconspicuously but crisply. You need to experiment to play this figure, called an Alberti Bass, to allow your wrist and hand to remain fluid and not to become tense. Practice and perform with no pedal for this movement. You must also retain a steady beat. We recommend you break your practice down into sections, practicing hands alone, then hands together, and working up to a performance tempo over time.

FRIEDRICH KUHLAU

German composer.
Born in Uelzen, Germany, September 11, 1786;
died in Copenhagen, March 12, 1832.

When he was a boy, Kuhlau fell on the ice and lost his right eye. Despite this physical handicap, he became a noted pianist and teacher in Hamburg. To avoid being forced to fight for Napoleon when the city of Hamburg was invaded in 1810, Kuhlau fled to Copenhagen, where he earned his living for the rest of his life, teaching and concertizing locally and throughout northern Europe. In 1831, he lost all of his unpublished works in a fire which left him in poor health until his death a year later from complications of smoke inhalation. Kuhlau was known during his life as a composer for the stage and for his many works for piano. Today his piano sonatinas are perennial favorites for student pianists.

Sonatina in C Major, Op. 55, No. 1

A steady beat and a refined touch will take you quite far in playing in Classical Era style. A refined touch does not, however, mean that everything is played the same. In this sonatina you need to make careful choices of articulation. Do not make the mistake of applying *legato* tone throughout. This would create a bland performance that is out of the style of the period. (The norm in the Classical period was to play *portato*, slightly separated, except for notes deliberately marked as slurred.) We have made occasional editorial suggestions about articulation that will help you find the style.

In the first movement, in the first measure in the right hand, a pianist needs to decide which notes are slurred. One choice is to slur the first two notes together, the second two notes, and the third two notes, making three two-note phrases. A slur over an entire measure is probably acceptable in measures 3–4 in the right hand. The first two beats of measure 5 should be played lightly with slight separation, not quite staccato. Experimenting with articulation, slurring, and staccato is fundamental to finding Classical style. Repeated notes, such as in measure 10 and the first two beats of measure 11, should be slightly separated. Notice in measure 10 that while the right hand is playing with separation, the left hand is playing eighth notes smoothly and quietly. Clarity is extremely important in Classical period style. You need to practice with no pedal, and possibly not add any pedal at all in performing this sonatina.

A sonatina is an abbreviated sonata form, and as sometimes is the case, this sonata only has two movements. The composer has essentially omitted the second movement and gone straight to a lively finale. The Vivace movement of this sonatina is a rondo form, which is common to the final movement of a sonata or sonatina. The rondo theme is stated in the first eight measures. We can find it restated again beginning in the pickups to measures 9, measure 37, measure 45, and measure 77. The rondo theme melody and rhythm are developed as a motive by the composer elsewhere in the movement. In Classical style, repeated notes should be played with gentle separation, not short, dry staccato. This occurs frequently in this movement, such as in measures 1–3, 9–11, etc. It is not very often that a composer asks for a chromatic scale in a Classical era piece. However, Kuhlau has written this, beginning in measure 25 and again in measure 97. This is an excellent opportunity for you to practice the chromatic scale as part of your warm up in preparing this sonatina. As with any scale work,

your aim should be evenness of tone and rhythm accomplished by efficient finger movement. Do not speed up during these chromatic scales. The section that begins in measure 53 is really the furthest departure from the rondo theme, with a left hand figure that creates a flowing motion. Notice that the composer has written sharp contrasts of dynamics. For instance, the first statement of the rondo theme is $\boldsymbol{p}$. Suddenly, without *crescendo*, we move to $\boldsymbol{f}$ at the end of measure 8. Again, suddenly, we move from $\boldsymbol{f}$ to $\boldsymbol{p}$ at the end of measure 16. These sharp, crisp contrasts in dynamics are essential in defining the style of the piece.

WOLFGANG AMADEUS MOZART
Austrian composer.
Born in Salzburg, January 27, 1756;
died in Vienna, December 5, 1791.

One of the greatest talents in the history of music, Mozart was first a child prodigy as a composer, keyboard player and violinist. He developed into a composer unrivalled by any, with a vast output in opera, symphonies, choral music, keyboard music and chamber music, all accomplished before his death at the young age of 35. Mozart spent most of his adult life living and working in Vienna. He was at the end of the era when successful musicians and composers attained substantial royal court appointments. A major position of this sort eluded him, despite his enormous talent, and he constantly sought opportunities to compose and perform. His music embodies the eighteenth century "age of reason" in its refined qualities, but adds playfulness, earnestness, sophistication and a deep sense of melody and harmony. Mozart's piano sonatas, concertos, sets of variations, and many other pieces at all levels from quite easy to virtuoso have become standards in the literature. His first compositions as a boy, from age 5, were for keyboard.

The notes on the individual pieces below were adapted from material previously published in *Mozart: 15 Intermediate Piano Pieces* (Schirmer Performance Editions).

Piece for Clavier in F Major, KV 33B
Mozart composed this piece in October of 1766 on the back of minutes for a meeting of the Zurich Collegium Musicum, which indicates that the ten-year-old boy genius might have been bored during some formality. He likely performed it in Zurich on October 6 and 9, 1766. The form of this

piece is ABA[1], with repeats, with the A section returning in abbreviated fashion in measure 19. Notice how the first eight notes of the melody are developed and used to construct the rest of the piece. This happy music requires a light, bouncing touch in the broken octaves in the left hand. Play the left hand with light separation. Notice the recommended articulation for the right hand melody, with some notes marked staccato and others in brief slurred groups. This piece should be played with no pedal.

Andantino in E-flat Major, KV 236 (588b)

This piece is Mozart's adaptation of "Non vi turbate," an aria from Christoph Willibald Gluck's opera *Alceste*. Mozart may have heard this aria in a performance of the opera given at Schönbrunn Castle in Vienna on December 3, 1781. Mozart's keyboard piece was probably written in 1783, possibly as a theme upon which variations would be based, though this has not been conclusively proven. Mozart's adaptation is in AB form, with repeats, and concentrates primarily on the Gluck's orchestral introduction and conclusion to the aria. Find a singing tone for the top voice melody, remembering the vocal origin of the piece. Play not with constant legato on every note, but using the recommended slurring. Imagine a soprano with the most beautiful voice in the world singing the top note melody of the right hand, and let that imagined voice inspire you.

Rondo in C Major, KV334 (320b)

This happy rondo is a piano arrangement, probably by the composer, of a movement from Mozart's Divertimento in D Major for strings and horns, which was likely written during the summer of 1780. The piece is a simple rondo in ABABA form. Editorial suggestions have been made in the articulations to imitate the orchestration of the original music. Imagine a how a violinist might phrase and articulate the treble melody of the opening line. Repeated notes, such as the G's in measure 1, should be played with light separation. Notice how Mozart playfully varies the theme when it recurs. Suggested sudden dynamic changes, appropriate to the period, will help make the music interesting. We recommend that you play this short piece with no pedal.

Adagio for Glass Harmonica, KV 356 (617a)

This haunting piece was written in early 1791 for Marianne Krichgeßner, the nearly blind glass harmonica player who gave the first performance of a version for glass harmonica, flute, oboe, violin, and cello on August 19, 1791 in Vienna. The glass harmonica uses a series of glass bowls or goblets to produce musical tones through friction. The ethereal ringing sound produced is similar to when you run your finger along the moistened edge of a drinking glass. (Benjamin Franklin invented a version of the glass harmonica in 1757, which he called an armonica.) This adagio is in ABA[1] form, with the second appearance of the A section melodically embellished in the right hand. Notice that the entire piece is written in the treble register. There is a gossamer quality to the music, which must be performed smoothly and sensitively, but with a steady tempo. While the glass harmonica was something of a novelty instrument, this earnest and touching composition for it, with its poignantly rich harmonic changes, is certainly not a novelty piece at all. Take care not to romanticize your performance too much. Retain a classical period restraint.

Funeral March for Signor Maestro Contrapunto, KV 453a

The march was composed in 1784 for Barbara Ployer, one of Mozart's students, to whom he also dedicated his Piano Concerto in E-flat Major, K. 449 and his Piano Concerto in G Major, K. 453. It is in AB form, with repeats. The title is a joke. Maestro Contrapunto means Master Counterpoint. Counterpoint, meaning the combination of two or more melodic lines, reached its compositional zenith during the Baroque period. Its profuse use fell out of favor as the *stile galante* movement took hold during the mid-eighteenth century, and simpler, leaner music became more widespread. Barbara Ployer also took lessons from Mozart in music theory. This march, which lacks any counterpoint itself, is a musical joke raised as a result of Ployer's theory lessons. Even in its novelty and humor it is still a beautifully conceived piece. Performing this march requires a solemn-faced solemnity similar to an actor playing a very serious (and ultimately very ironic) role in a comedy. The piece is very dramatic, with many *subito* changes in dynamics. Taper the two-note slurs carefully at the end of each main section.

German Dance in C Major, KV 605, No. 3

This piece is an arrangement of one of the three German dances Mozart wrote for orchestra early in 1791, the last year of his life. The form of this piece is ABCDAB, with repeats. When performing this music, remember its orchestral origins and produce a full, rounded tone. The repeated eighth notes should always have dynamic direction, gradually and subtly increasing in volume. Notice the recommended articulation in the right hand in measures 5–8. To find true Classical Era style use a mixture of tasteful articulation (staccato and short, two note slurs), rather than playing all the notes the same. In the original version for orchestra, Mozart introduces sleigh bells in the trio section (thus the name "The Sleighride" for this section). The trio section should be played smoothly, contrasting with the texture of the first page of music. Think of the trio section as gently gliding along, as a sleigh glides through the snow.

—Richard Walters, editor
Joshua Parman, assistant editor

German Dance in G Major

Ludwig van Beethoven
WoO 8, No. 6

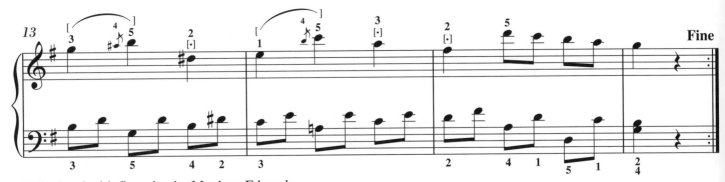

Edited and with fingering by Matthew Edwards.
Editorial suggestions are in brackets.

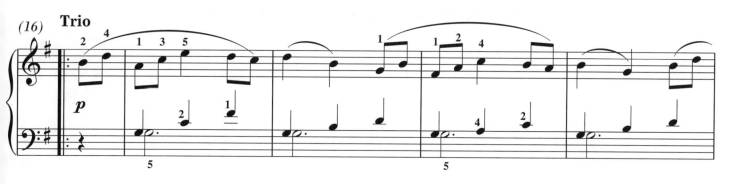

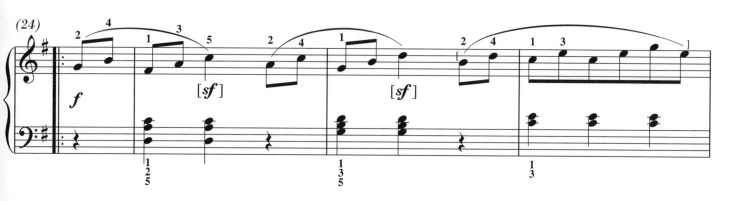

D.C. al Fine
senza repetizione

Andantino in E-flat Major

Adaptation of an aria* by Christoph Willibald Gluck

Wolfgang Amadeus Mozart
KV 236 (588b)

* "Non vi turbate" from *Alceste*.
Edited and with fingering by Elena Abend.
Editorial suggestions are in brackets.

Piece for Clavier in F Major
(Klavierstück)

Wolfgang Amadeus Mozart
KV 33B

Edited and with fingering by Elena Abend.
Editorial suggestions are in brackets.

[poco rit. 2nd time]

German Dance in C Major

Ludwig van Beethoven
WoO 8, No. 7

Edited and with fingering by Matthew Edwards.
Editorial suggestions are in brackets.

(16) **Trio**

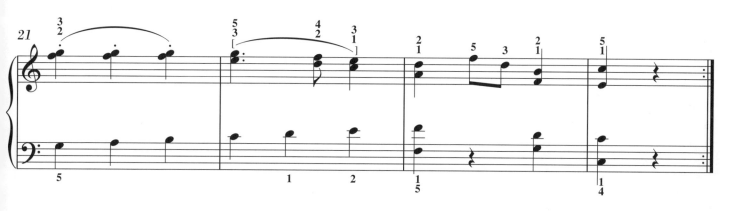

D.C. al Fine
senza repetizione

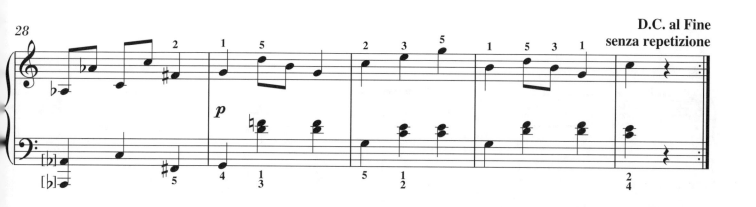

German Dance in B-flat Major

Ludwig van Beethoven
WoO 13, No. 2

[**Allegro moderato**]

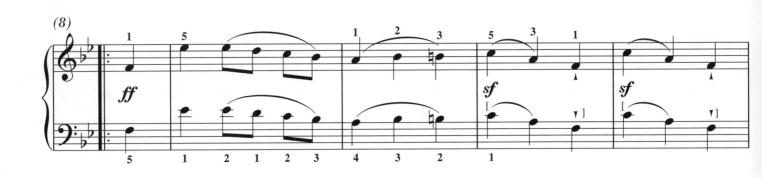

Edited and with fingering by Matthew Edwards.

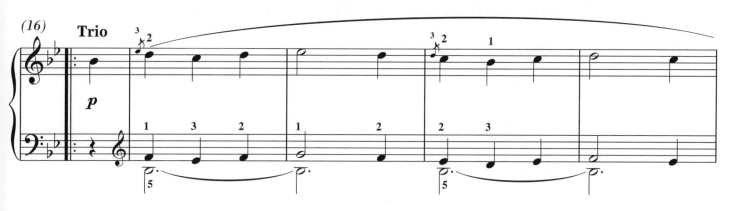

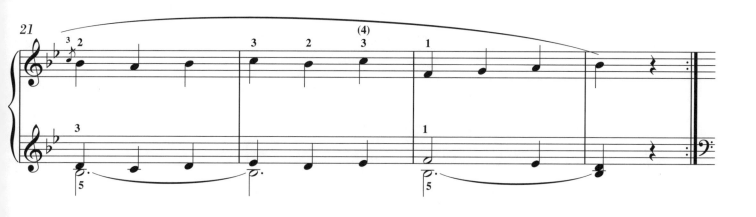

D.C. al Fine
senza repetizione

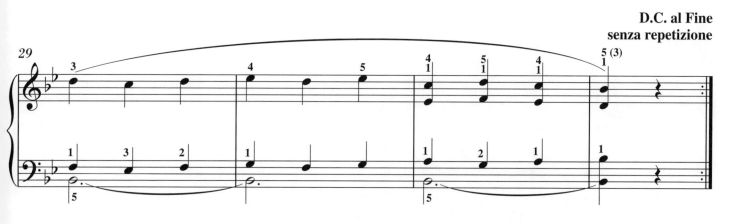

LABORUM
DULCE
LENIMEN

G. SCHIRMER

Funeral March for Signor Maestro Contrapunto

Wolfgang Amadeus Mozart
KV 453a

Edited and with fingering by Elena Abend.
Editorial suggestions are in brackets.

Adagio for Glass Harmonica

Wolfgang Amadeus Mozart
KV 356 (617a)

Edited and with fingering by Elena Abend.
Editorial suggestions are in brackets.

German Dance in C Major

Wolfgang Amadeus Mozart
KV 605, No. 3

[Allegro ♩. = ca. 52-56]

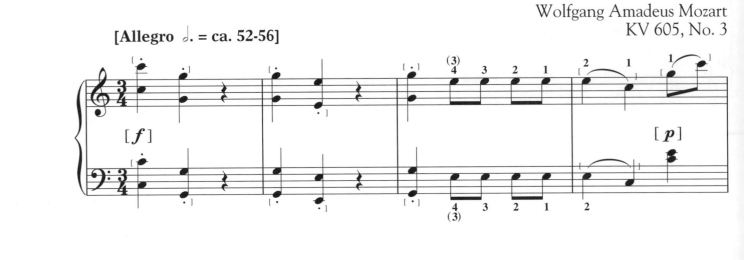

Fine

Eliminate repeats on the Da Capo.
Edited and with fingering by Elena Abend.
Editorial suggestions are in brackets.

Trio (The Sleighride)

D.C. al Fine
second time

Rondo in C Major

Wolfgang Amadeus Mozart
KV 334 (320b)

Edited and with fingering by Elena Abend.
Editorial suggestions are in brackets.

Sonatina in C Major

I

Friedrich Kuhlau
Op. 55, No. 1

Allegro [♩ = ca. 88]

Edited and with fingering by Jennifer Linn.
Editorial suggestions are in brackets.

II

Sonatina in C Major

I

Anton Diabelli
Op. 168, No. 3

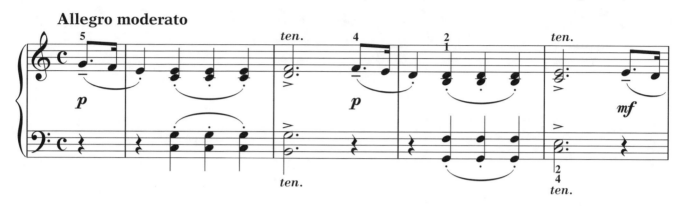

Fingering by Matthew Edwards.

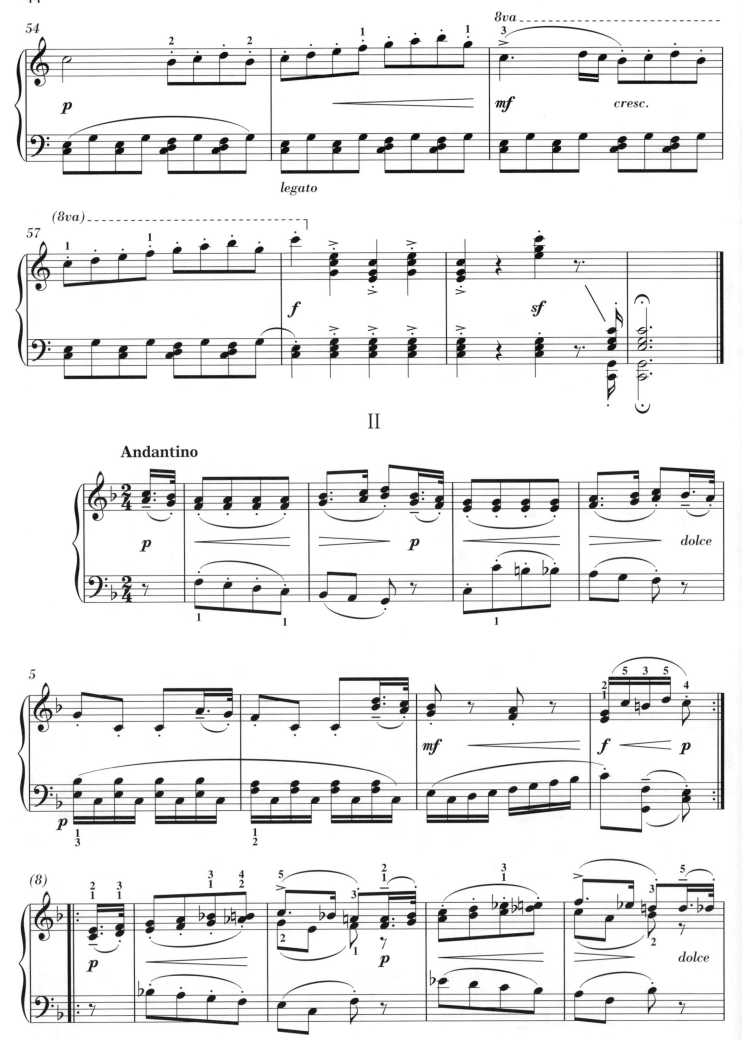

II

Andantino

Allegro
from Sonata in C Major

Franz Joseph Haydn
Hob. XVI/1

Fingering by Stefanie Jacob.

Sonatina in G Major

I

Jan Ladislav Dussek
Op. 20, No. 1

Allegro non tanto [♩ = 132]

*All notes with the accent ⸜ should be played very short, though as part of the melodic material.
Staccato indications exist in measures 17 and 19 only. These should be played lightly.
Edited and with fingering by Jeffrey Biegel.

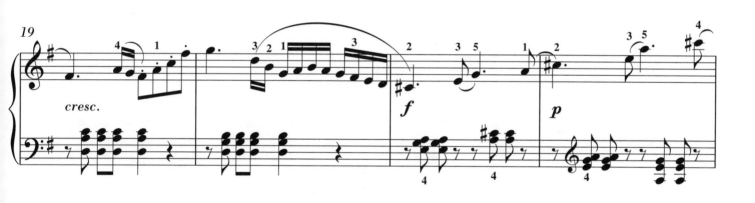

II

RONDO

Allegretto–Tempo di Minuetto [♪ = 126]

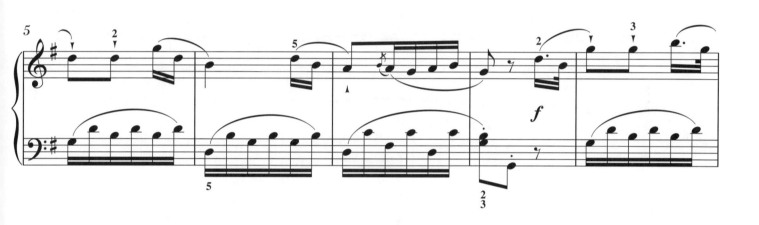

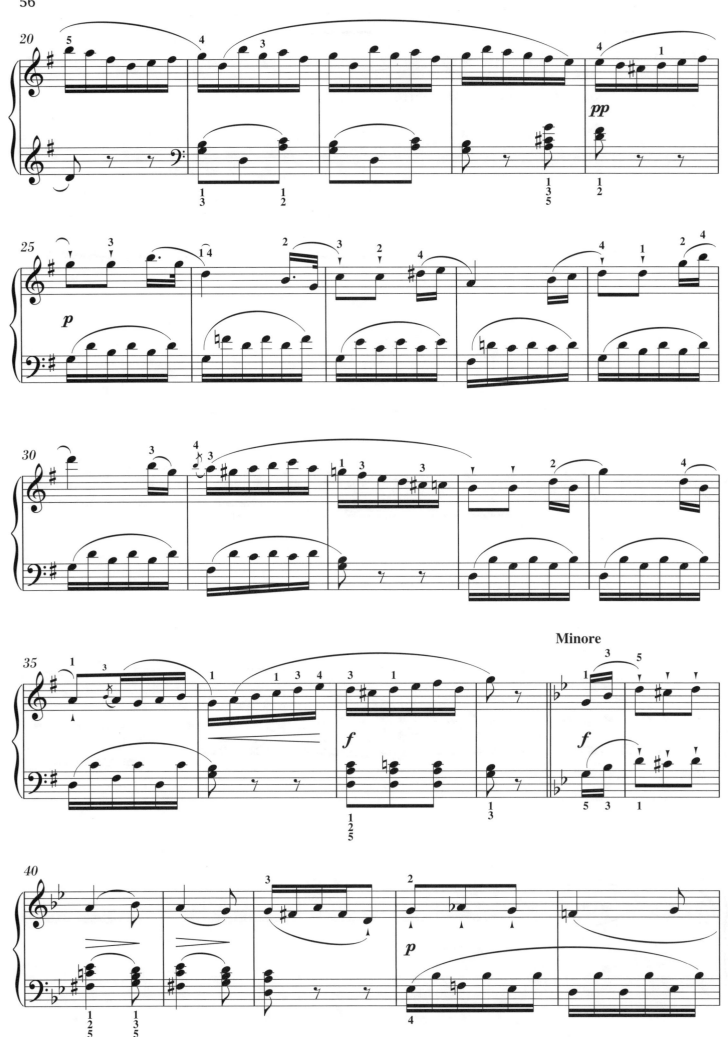

Minore

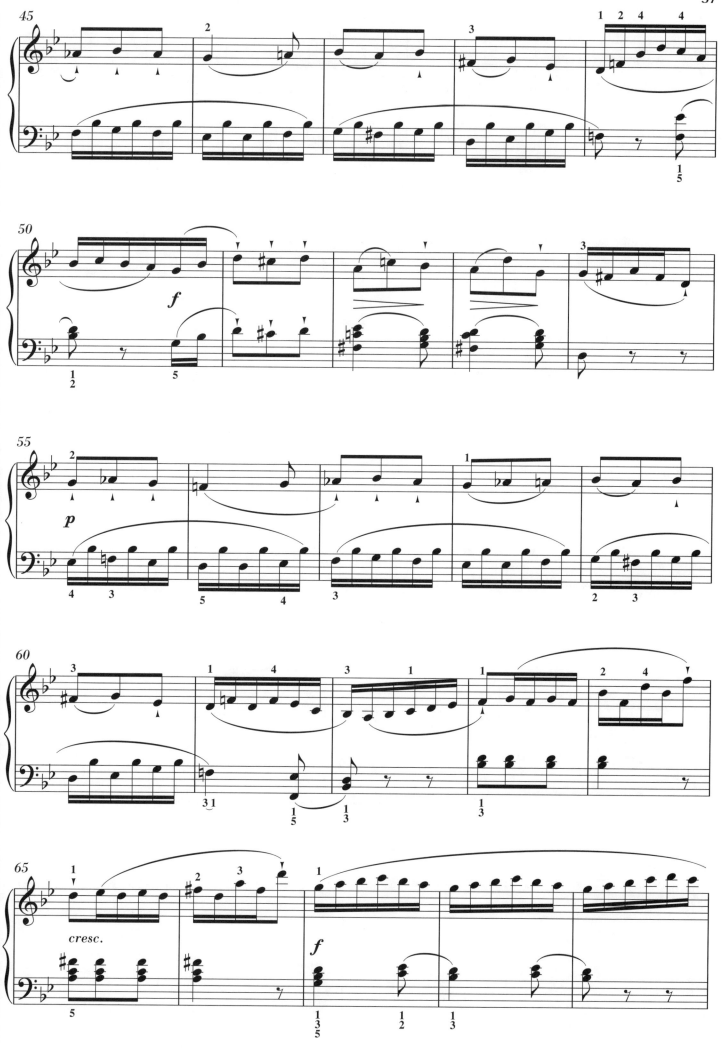

f or *p* (editor)

Solfeggietto in C minor

Carl Philipp Emanuel Bach
H. 220

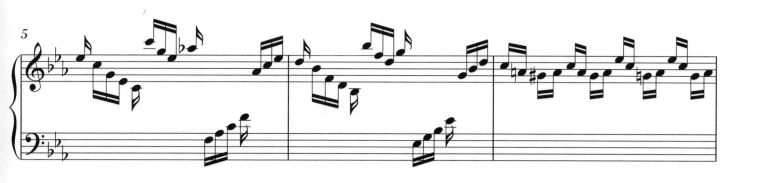

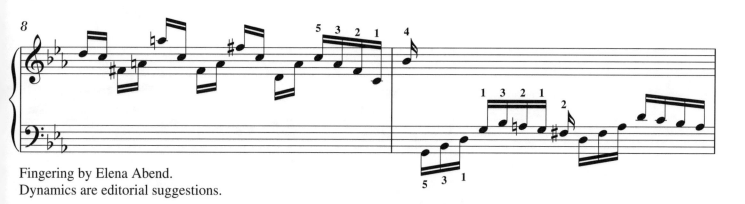

Fingering by Elena Abend.
Dynamics are editorial suggestions.

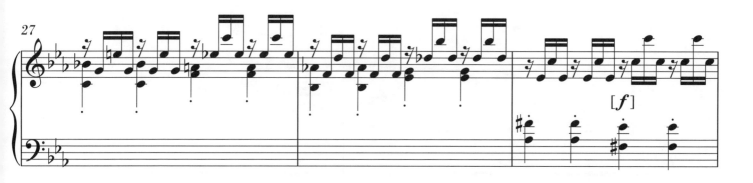

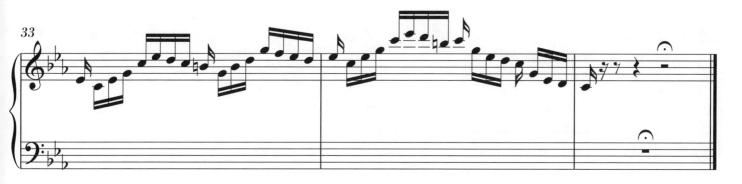

Sonatina in F Major

I

Muzio Clementi
Op. 36, No. 4

Edited and with fingering by Jennifer Linn.

II

Andante con espressione [♩ = 46–64]

III

RONDO

Allegro vivace [♩ = 72–88]

ABOUT THE EDITOR

RICHARD WALTERS

Richard Walters is a pianist, composer, and editor of hundred of publications in a long music publishing career. He is Vice President of Classical Publications at Hal Leonard, and directs a variety of publications for piano, voice, and solo instruments. Walters directs all publishing in the Schirmer Performance Editions series. Among other piano publications, he is editor of the revised edition of *Samuel Barber: Complete Piano Music, Leonard Bernstein: Music for Piano,* and the multi-volume series *The World's Great Classical Music*. His editing credits for vocal publications include *Samuel Barber: 65 Songs, Benjamin Britten: Collected Songs, Benjamin Britten: Complete Folksong Arrangements, Leonard Bernstein: Art Songs and Arias, The Purcell Collection: Realizations by Benjamin Britten, Bernstein Theatre Songs, G. Schirmer Collection of American Art Song,* 28 *Italian Songs and Arias for the Seventeenth and Eighteenth Centuries,* 80 volumes of standard repertoire in the Vocal Library series, and the multi-volume *The Singer's Musical Theatre Anthology*. Walters has published dozens of various arrangements, particularly for voice and piano, and is the composer of nine song cycles. He was educated with a bachelor's degree in piano at Simpson College, where he studied piano with Robert Larsen and composition with Sven Lekberg, and graduate studies in composition at the University of Minnesota, where he studied with Dominick Argento.